PIANO/VOCAL/CHORDS

MARVIN GAYE
GREATEST HITS

ISBN 0-7935-7567-2

HAL•LEONARD®
CORPORATION
7777 W. BLUEMOUND RD. P.O. BOX 13819 MILWAUKEE, WI 53213

Visit Hal Leonard Online at
www.halleonard.com

WHAT'S GOING ON

Words and Music by
MARVIN GAYE, AL CLEVELAND
and RENALDO BENSON

2. Father, father we don't need to escalate
You see, war is not the answer for only love can conquer hate
You know we've got to find a way to bring some lovin' here today. (Chorus)

3. Father, father everybody thinks we're wrong
Oh but, who are they to judge us simply because our hair is **long?**
Oh you know we've got to find a way bring some understanding **here today. (Chorus)**

I HEARD IT THROUGH THE GRAPEVINE

Words and Music by
NORMAN WHITFIELD and
BARRETT STRONG

3. People say believe half of what you see
Oh, and none of what you hear;
But I can't help but be confused
If it's true please tell me dear.
Do you plan to let me go
For the other guy you loved before?

DANCING IN THE STREET

Words and Music by
MARVIN GAYE, IVY HUNTER
and WILLIAM STEVENSON

G♯7
re-cords play-ing, dan - cing in the street oh, it does - n't mat-ter what
re-cords play-ing, dan - cing in the street oh, it does - n't mat-ter what
C♯m
F♯m
you wear just as long as you are there, so come on ev - 'ry guy
you wear just as long as you are there, so come on ev - 'ry guy
B7sus
E
grab a girl ev - 'ry-where a-round the world. They'll be danc - ing
grab a girl ev - 'ry-where a-round the world. They'll be danc - ing
1.
E
they're dan-cin' in the street. (Dan-cing in the street.) This is an way down in L. A.
they're dan-cin' in the street. (Dan-cing in the street.)
ev-ry day they're dan-cing in the street. (Dan-cing in the street.) Here comes a big strong man.
Get in time dan-cing in the street. (Dan-cing in the street.) A-cross the o-cean blue
me and you we're dan-cing in the street.
(fade)

AIN'T NO MOUNTAIN HIGH ENOUGH

Words and Music by
NICKOLAS ASHFORD and
VALERIE SIMPSON

2. I set you free
I told you you could always count on me
From that day on, I made a vow,
I'll be there when you want me,
Some way, some how.
'Cause baby there (Chorus)

3. My love is alive
Way down in my heart
Although we are miles apart
If you ever need a helping hand,
I'll be there on the double
As fast as I can.
Don't you know that there (Chorus)

THAT'S THE WAY LOVE IS

Words and Music by
NORMAN WHITFIELD
and BARRETT STRONG

Ab7
love is babe,
love is hon - ey,
(that's the way love is Sho' nuff' how it is) Oh
(that's the way love is Sho' nuff' how it is) Oh
Ebm7
that's the way
that's the way
love is, shook up,
love is, ba - by
Ab7
(that's the way love is Sho'
(that's the way love is Sho'
To Coda
Ebm
1.
nuff how it is) that's how it is.
nuff how it is) that's how it is.
Wo
that's how it is hon - ey
Ebm
2.
Oh
Ebm
ba-by

3. Oh, listen to me little darlin'
The road of love gets rough sometimes
Don't let it get the best of you.
Said I've been hurt by love so many times
So I know just what you're going through
Oh, you wish that you were never born
You better forget him now that he's gone;
Just remember, that's the way love is babe
That's the way love is. Sho' nuff how it is
Oh, that's the way love is, honey,
That's the way love is. Sho' nuff how it is
That's how it is.

HOW SWEET IT IS
(To Be Loved By You)

Words and Music by
BRIAN HOLLAND,
LAMONT DOZIER and
EDDIE HOLLAND

How Sweet It Is - 3 - 1

G
Em
D7
I need-ed some-one to un-der - stand my ups and downs, there you were,
Ev - 'ry-thing I did was just a bore; ev - 'ry-where I went, seems I've
C
G
C
To Coda
with sweet love and de - vo - tion,
been there be-fore, but you bright-en up for me all of my days
Em
D
C
G
deep-ly touch-ing my e - mo - tion.
with a love so sweet in so man-y ways
I want to stop and thank you,
C
G
C
ba - by; I want to stop and thank you ba - by, yes, I do;
1.2.
D. C. al Coda
(after 2nd ending)

Coda
G
C
You were bet-ter to me than I was to my-self, for
Em
D
C
G
me there's you and there ain't no - bo - dy else. I want to stop and thank you
C
G
C
ba - by; I want to stop and thank you ba - by, yes I do,
C
Am7
(D Bass)
Am
G
repeat and fade
How sweet it is to be loved by you.

TOO BUSY THINKING ABOUT MY BABY

Words and Music by
JANIE BRADFORD,
NORMAN WHITFIELD and
BARRETT STRONG

B♭maj7
Am
B♭maj7
grow, ain't nev - er give it a thought to
B♭maj7
Gm7
F
Gm
F
Gm
F
where riv - ers flow.
Gm7
F
Ain't got time for noth - in' else.
F
Gm
F
Gm
F
Gm
F
I ain't got time to dis - cuss the weath - er, or know what's go - ing

Gm7 F Gm F Gm F
on, and I ain't got time to do no stud - y - ing
Gm F Gm7 F Am
once I get out of class. And I'm just a
B♭maj7 Am B♭maj7
fel - low with a one track mind, and when it
Am B♭maj7 B♭maj7 Gm
comes to think - in' a - bout an - y - thing but my ba - by, I just don't have time.

F Gm F Gm F Gm7 F
Fine
Ain't got time for noth - in' else.
F Gm F Gm F Gm F
I ain't got time to read a news - pa - per or look at T.
Gm F Gm F Gm F
V. 'Cause I'm not con - cerned with what the fu - ture holds
Gm F Gm Am Asus
D.S. al Fine
in store for me. I'm just a

YOU'RE ALL I NEED TO GET BY

Words and Music by
NICKOLAS ASHFORD
and VALERIE SIMPSON

D7
Fm
(Boy) And when I lose my will you'll be there to push me up the hill. There's
(Boy) I know you can make a man out of a soul that did-n't have a goal. 'Cause
Chorus
C F C F C F6 C D7 Fm
no, no look-ing back for us, we got love sure 'nough, that's e-nough. You're
we, we got the right found-a-tion and with love and de-ter-mi-na-tion. You're
1. C F C Fm C Fm G7+ 2. C
all, You're All I Need To Get By. I all, you're all I
F C F
want to strive for and do a lit-tle more. All, all the joys un-der the sun wrapp'd up in-to one. You're
C Bb7 A7 Fm6 G9 G7-9 (Sus 4) C D7 Fm6 C6
all, You're All I Need To Get By.
play 3 times
rit.

PRIDE AND JOY

Words and Music by
NORMAN WHITFIELD, MARVIN GAYE
and WILLIAM STEVENSON

B♭7 (Add D♭)
F7 (Add A♭)
all my mon-ey; and that's why you are my pride and
whole darn town; and that's why I be-lieve you're my pride and
B♭
to Coda
F7
B♭7 (Add D♭)
joy; and I'm tell-ing the world you're my (pride and joy,) pride and
joy;
E♭7
joy, (pride and joy,) I be-lieve I'm your (ba - by boy,) ba - by
B♭
boy, (ba - by boy.) and I know that you're my (pride and joy,) pride and

F7
D.C. al Coda
joy (pride and joy,) yeah ba - by, (ba - by boy,) yeah ba - by (ba - by boy,)
F7
B♭7
Coda
yeah, yeah, yeah. Yeah, (pride and joy,) yeah yeah, (pride and joy,) yeah,
E♭7
(pride and joy,) (pride and joy,) ah (ba - by boy,) ba - by
fade 2nd time
B♭7
F7
boy, (ba - by boy,) oo (pride and joy,) my pride and joy, (pride and joy,) and I love you like a ba -
C7
F7
B♭
B♭ (D Bass)
C♯dim
Cm7
B♭
by loves his toy. Yeah, yeah, yeah.

GOT TO GIVE IT UP
(Part 1)

Words and Music by
MARVIN GAYE

D7
E7
But my bod - y yearned to be
Long as you're groov - in' there's al - ways a chance
A7
B7
D7
free.
I got up on the floor, boy,
some - bod - y watch - in'
E7
A7
B7
(Repeat Twice)
so some - bod-y could choose me.
might wan - na make ro - mance.
No more
Move your
(Repeat Twice)
A7
Move it up,
Turn it round,

ooh, shake it down, Ooh,
Am7
you can bump me when you want to, babe.
Dm7
This is such a groov - y par - ty, ba - by. Danc - in'
face to face and ev - ery- bod - y's scream-in'

this is such a groov - y place.
Am7
All the young la - dies are so fine.
A7
D7
You're mov - in' your bod - y
E7
A7
B7
leaves me with no doubt;
know what you're think -

3. Move your body, move baby, and dance all night,
To the groovin', I feel all right.
Havin' a party, ooh, invite all your friends;
But if you see me stop by, let me in.
Baby, just party all night long.
Let me slip into your erotic zone.
(We heard that!)

(Extra Lyrics for Ad Lib Ending)
Keep on dancin', oh keep on dancin'.
Ooh, look so good, yeah, keep on dancin'.
Oh, now sugar, got to give it up.
Keep on dancin', gotta give it up.
Keep on dancin' . . . .

LET'S GET IT ON

Words and Music by
MARVIN GAYE and
ED TOWNSEND

E♭ Gm A♭ B♭7 E♭ Gm A♭ B♭7
since we got to be let's live. I love you.
E♭ Gm A♭ B♭7 E♭ Gm A♭ B♭7
There's no-thin' wrong with me lov-in' you, Ba-by, no, no. And
E♭ Gm A♭ B♭7 E♭ Gm
giv-in' your-self to me can nev-er be wrong if the love is true. Oh, ba - by,
A♭ B♭7 A♭ E♭ Gm
ooh. Don't you know how sweet and won-der-ful life can be. Ooh,
A♭ E♭7 A♭ E♭ Gm
ooh. I'm ask - in' you, ba - by, to get it on with me. Ooh, ooh,

Ab Bb7 Ab Eb Gm
ooh. I ain't goin' to wor - ry. I ain't goin' to push. I won't push you, ba
Ab Bb Ab Fm
by. Just come on, come on, come on, come on, come on ba - by, stop beat-in' 'round the
Bb7 Eb Gm Ab Bb7
bush. Hey, Let's Get It On. Ooh, ooh. Let's Get It
Eb Gm Ab Bb7 Eb Gm Ab Bb7
On. You know what I'm talk-in' a-bout. Come on, ba - by. Hey, hey, Let your love come.
Eb Gm Ab Bb7 Eb Gm Ab Bb7
out. If you be-lieve in love, Let's Get It On. Ooh. Let's Get It On, ba-
Eb Gm Ab Bb7 Eb Gm Ab Bb7
by, this min - ute. Oh, yeah, Let's Get It On. Ee, please

Eb Gm Ab Bb7 Ab
get it on. Hey, hey.
Come on, come on, come on, come on, come on, dar-
Fm Bb7 Eb Gm
lin', Stop beat-in' 'round the bush.
Oh, gon - na get it on.
Right with you,
Ab Bb7 Eb Gm Ab Bb7
ba - by, I want to get it on.
You don't have to wor - ry that it's wrong.
Eb Gm Ab Bb7 Eb Gm
If the spi - rit moves you, let me groove you.
Good, let your love come down, oh.
Ab Bb7 Eb Gm Ab Bb7 Eb Gm
Get It On. Come on, ba - by.
Do you know I mean it? I've been sanc-ti-fied.
(fade)
Hey,
Ab Bb Eb Gm Ab Bb7 Eb
hey. Girl, you give me good feel - ings, so good,
some-thin' like sum-mer-time.

MERCY MERCY ME
(The Ecology)

Words and Music by
MARVIN GAYE

1. Ah things ain't what they used to be, no, no
Oil wasted on the ocean and upon
Our seas fish full of mercury, Ah.

2. Ah things ain't what they used to be
What about this over crowded land
How much more abuse from man can she stand?

AIN'T NOTHING LIKE THE REAL THING

Words and Music by
NICKOLAS ASHFORD and
VALERIE SIMPSON

Abmaj7 G Cm7
it can't see or come to me when I call your name. I
Bbm7 Bbm (Eb Bass) Ab Eb (G Bass) Fm Eb Ab (Bb Bass)
re - al - ize it's just a pic - ture in - side a frame. 2.) I read your
Eb Fm7 Eb (G Bass) Abmaj7 G
let - ters when you're not near me, but they don't move me, and they don't groove me like
Cm7 Bbm7 Bbm (Eb Bass) Ab Eb (G Bass) Fm
when I hear your sweet voice whis - per - ing

3. I play the game, a fantasy.
I pretend I'm not in reality.
I need the shelter of your arms to comfort me.

4. I got some memories to look back on
And though they help me when you phone,
I'm well aware nothin' can take the place of you being there.

SEXUAL HEALING

Words and Music by
MARVIN GAYE, ODELL BROWN
and DAVID RITZ

Moderate half time feel (𝅗𝅥 = 1 beat)

G Am Em7 F C
B♭ Cm Gm7 A♭ E♭
Ba - by, I'm hot just like an ov - en; I need some lov - in'.
Ba - by, I got sick this morn- in', A sea was storm - in' in - side of me.
G Am Em7 F C
B♭ Cm Gm7 A♭ E♭
Ba - by, I can't hold it much long - er; It's get - tin' strong - er and strong - er.
Ba - by, I think I'm cap - siz - in', The waves are ris - in' and ris - in'. And

G Am Em7 F C
B♭ Cm Gm7 A♭ E♭
When I get that feel - in' I want sex - u - al heal - ing,
When I get that feel - in' I want sex - u - al heal - ing,
G Am Em7 F C
B♭ Cm Gm7 A♭ E♭
sex - u - al heal - ing. Oh ba - by,
sex - u - al heal - ing. (It's good for me)
G Am Em7 F C
B♭ Cm Gm7 A♭ E♭
makes me feel so fine,
makes me feel so fine, (It's sumpcherous)
G Am Em7 F C
B♭ Cm Gm7 A♭ E♭
Helps to re - lieve my mind.
Helps to re - lieve my mind. (And it's good for us)

G Am Em7 F C
B♭ Cm Gm7 A♭ E♭
Sex - u - al healing baby is good for me.
Sex - u - al healing baby is good for me.
G Am Em7 Dm7 Em7 Fmaj7 F/G
B♭ Cm Gm7 Fm7 Gm7 A♭maj7 A♭/B♭
To Coda
Sex - u - al healing is something that's good for me.
Sex - u - al healing is something that's good for me.
C E7
E♭ G7
Whenever blue tear drops are falling
Fmaj7 Dm7 Em7 Fmaj7 F/G C
A♭maj7 Fm7 Gm7 A♭maj7 A♭/B♭ E♭
And my e - mo - tion - al sta - bil - i - ty is leav - ing

E7
G7
me There is some - thing I can do: I can
Fmaj7
A♭maj7
Dm7
Fm7
Em7
Gm7
Fmaj7
A♭maj7
F/G
A♭/B♭
C
E♭
get on the tel - e - phone and call you up, ba - by. Say
E7
G7
Hon - ey, I know you'll be there to re - lieve me 'cause the
Fmaj7
A♭maj7
Dm7
Fm7
Em7
Gm7
Fmaj7
A♭maj7
F/G
A♭/B♭
C
E♭
love you give to me will be.

E7
G7
If you don't know the thing you're deal - ing, I
Fmaj7
Abmaj7
Dm7
Fm7
Em7
Gm7
Fmaj7
Abmaj7
F/G
Ab/Bb
can tell you dar - lin', that it's sex - u - al heal - ing.
G
Bb
Am
Cm
Em7
Gm7
F
Ab
C
Eb
Get up, get up, get up, get up, Let's make love to - night!
G
Bb
Am
Cm
Em7
Gm7
F
Ab
C
Eb
D.S. al Coda
Wake up, wake up, wake up, wake up, 'cause you do it right!

Coda
C
E♭
E7
G7
And it's good for me,
And it's so good
Fmaj7
A♭maj7
Dm7
Fm7
Em7
Gm7
to me, my ba - by.
Oh
Fmaj7
A♭maj7
F/G
A♭/B♭
C
E♭
E7
G7
Oh, come take con - trol
Just grab a hold
Fmaj7
A♭maj7
of my bod - y and mind;
Soon we'll be

Dm7 Em7 Fmaj7 F/G C
Fm7 Gm7 A♭maj7 A♭/B♭ E♭
mak - in' it hon - ey, Oh, we'll be do - in', fine. You're my med -
E7
G7
e - cine, O - pen up and let me in.
Fmaj7 Dm7 Em7
A♭maj7 Fm7 Gm7
Dar - lin', you're so pret - ty, I can't wait for you to
Fmaj7 F/G G Am Em7
A♭maj7 A♭/B♭ B♭ Cm Gm7
op - er - ate.
(heavy breathing..................................)

F C G Am
A♭ E♭ B♭ Cm
Let's make love to - night!
Wake up, wake up,
Em7 F C
Gm7 A♭ E♭
wake up, wake up,
'cause you do it right!
G Am Em7 F C
B♭ Cm Gm7 A♭ E♭
(vocal improvisations)
G Am Em7 F C
B♭ Cm Gm7 A♭ E♭
Repeat and fade

R&R/Friday, April 6, 1984

On The Records

KEN BARNES

The Magnificent Marvin Gaye

Marvin Gaye, alone among his contemporaries, dominated three decades of popular music, playing a key role in determining the direction of pop and black music in the '60s, '70s, and '80s. As a singer, he was unmatchable, shifting easily from silky-smooth balladry to gritty raw soul to dazzling flights of interpretive artistry. As a stylistic model, he was the epitome of cool, from his sharpsuited sixties image to the eccentric but still commanding figure of recent days.

The early stylish image

An early record appearance

And as a songwriter, Gaye ranged as widely as any contemporary composer. There were the solid dance grooves of "Hitch Hike" and "Dancing In The Streets" (which he co-wrote for Martha & the Vandellas, who had earlier made their Motown debut backing him up on his first hit, "Stubborn Kind Of Fellow"). His "What's Going On" album in 1971 was a searching examination of political and ecological concerns. And "Let's Get It On" and, later, "Sexual Healing" were almost hymnlike testaments to the joys and curative powers of sex.

Marquees & Moonglows

Born in Washington, DC and trained to sing in the church, Gaye was in a mid-'50s vocal group called the **Rainbows**, along with future soul stars **Don Covay** and **Billy Stewart**. He later joined the **Marquees**, who became proteges of blues great **Bo Diddley** and recorded for **Okeh Records**. Next, he met Detroit R&B fixture **Harvey Fuqua** and joined up in a latter-day edition of Fuqua's famed doowop group the **Moonglows**, who were already past their "Sincerely" and "Ten Commandments Of Love" prime. Gaye sang lead on one of their releases, "Mama Loocie."

Through Fuqua he met the Motown family, and entered the organization as a session drummer, playing on early records by the **Miracles** and others. Convincing **Berry Gordy Jr.** he could sing, Gaye made three singles in 1961-62, none successful. But "Stubborn Kind Of Fellow" in late 1962 broke through, and Gaye refined its raw R&B approach with bigger hits like "Pride And Joy," the near-gospel "Can I Get A Witness," and "You're A Wonderful One."

Continued on Page 28

The Magnificent Marvin Gaye

Continued from Page 27

Explorations And Duets

In late 1964 "How Sweet It Is" became Gaye's biggest hit to date and added a new, midtempo, broader-appeal style to his arsenal. He was also refining a tough rock-oriented sound on "Baby Don't You Do It" – later covered by the **Who** and the **Band** – "Ain't That Peculiar," "One More Heartache," "Take This Heart Of Mine," and the remarkable "I'll Be Doggone," which assimilated the British Invasion's guitar innovations into the Motown sound. In addition, he did albums of standards, Broadway tunes, and **Nat Cole** songs, further establishing his versatility.

Duetting the public's appetite

Also in 1964, Gaye was teamed up with **Mary Wells**, the first in a series of duet partners. The double-sided hit "What's The Matter With You Baby"/"Once Upon A Time" helped establish the R&B male/female duet tradition (still strong today) and paved the way for Gaye duet hits with **Kim Weston** ("It Takes Two"), **Diana Ross** ("My Mistake"), and most memorably, **Tammi Terrell**. Gaye had ten hits with Terrell, including "Ain't No Mountain High Enough," "Ain't Nothing Like The Real Thing," and "Your Precious Love"; tragically, she died in his arms onstage in 1970, from a brain tumor.

While the spotlight was on Gaye's duet hits, his solo momentum slowed (he released just three singles between mid-1966 and the end of 1968). Then he delivered a streamlined, taut rendition of a song **Gladys Knight & the Pips** had hit with a year previous, "I Heard It Through The Grapevine," and it soared to the top of the charts, becoming one of Motown's alltime best-sellers.

In 1971 Gaye completed his concept album "What's Going On," and its political commentary and ethereal sound reportedly caused Motown to consider rejecting it. Once issued, however, it put Gaye, along with **Curtis Mayfield** and **Sly Stone**, in the vanguard of black musical activism. If "Mercy Mercy Me (The Ecology)" was a bit contrived, "Inner City Blues" and the LP's title track were eloquent and elegant expressions of discontent.

Gaye's first solo lead vocal

Gaye applied the same lyricism to erotic matters with "Let's Get It On" in 1973, "You Sure Love To Ball" in 1974, and "I Want You" the next year. His last big Motown hit was the live "Got To Give It Up" in 1977, which became a Black radio classic in its full-length version.

Ego Tripping And Healing

A confused artistic period ensued for Gaye, summed up by the titles of two of his nonhit singles, "Ego Tripping Out" and "Funky Space Reincarnation." Owing alimony to his ex-wife, Berry Gordy's sister **Anna**, he recorded a double album, assigned the royalties to her, and called it "Here, My Dear." Tax problems forced him to relocate to Europe, where he recorded his last Motown album, "In Our Lifetime." Motown remixed it, Gaye became upset, and began negotiations to leave the label, resulting in his signing with **Columbia** in 1982. (However, he remained on cordial enough terms with his alma mater to appear on the "Motown 25" TV special last year.)

The first Motown release, 1961

His first Columbia release, "Sexual Healing," displayed a new melodic grace and maturity that promised great things to come, and it was the smash comeback hit he needed as well. He also gained attention for a highly personalized version of the "Star Spangled Banner" delivered before an NBA playoff game, and made a generally triumphant return to live performance in 1983.

Now one of the greatest singers of the past 20 years is gone. The magnificence of his musical legacy is a consolation, but the promise of further greatness that won't now be kept makes his death more upsetting. Marvin Gaye was our pride and joy, and we'll miss him.